IMAGINE THAT

AN EXERCISE IN VISUALIZATION
AND CREATIVE THINKING

LUCE & BROWN
PUBLICATIONS

ABOUT THE AUTHOR

James Brown is a creative director specializing in branding, design, and advertising. With more than 15 years in the field, he has provided services to international franchise networks, multi-brand holding companies, small businesses, educational institutions, and nonprofits. He holds an AAS in Commercial Art & Advertising From Texas State Technical College and a BA in Visual Communications with a concentration in advertising from Savannah College of Art & Design. Over the years he has received more than 25 American Advertising Federation awards for illustration and design, and has been a member of the Visual Communication Technology advisory board at TSTC since 2008.

James currently resides in Fort Worth, Texas with his wife and daughter and enjoys woodworking, painting, and illustration in his spare time.

INTRODUCTION

Creativity can be defined as the ability to transcend traditional ideas, rules, and patterns to create meaningful new ideas, forms, and methods. In essence it equates to originality through the use of imagination.

As a creative director, I've found that one of the most effective ways to improve creativity and problem solving is through visualization. When you can look at a challenge and imagine the different possible outcomes before applying any effort you save time, energy, and in some cases money.

This book is an exercise in visualization and creative problem solving through drawing exercises. It is designed to promote creative thinking and is a method sometimes used in illustration education to encourage students to look at subject matter from a different perspective. Artistic ability is not the point here though. It doesn't matter if you can or cannot draw. The point of this book is to give you a task that would normally be easy, throw in a challenge, and then encourage you to make the challenge part of the solution. This method has not only helped me solve design solutions more effectively but it has trained me to approach almost any challenge in life by assessing my boundaries and then visualizing solutions that fit.

With practice, anyone can become good at visualization. This book helps train your brain to look for unseen opportunities to difficult challenges. By constantly pushing yourself to imagine different solutions you're likely to become more comfortable and experienced at it.

INSTRUCTIONS

Each page in this book has a word at the top. Somewhere else on the page is an oddly shaped line. The objective of this exercise is to draw whatever the word at the top of the page says using the line somehow in the drawing.

The lines are designed to go against the standard and often boring first mental image people associate with the word on the page. This is where the visualization comes in. If you have trouble determining how the line fits in with the subject, look at how the line fits in with a setting that has the subject in it. For example: If the prompt says "scissors" and you can't see how the line fits into the shape of scissors, you could use it to work with the outline of a piece of paper that the scissors are cutting. Try to think of way to incorporate the line as part of the subject first but if you can't, build it into a relevant setting. Don't assume you have to include the entire object on the page either. Your drawing could be just a cropped section or portion of the subject and the rest of it runs off the page. Use your imagination and try to visualize different ways the line could fit in the picture. If you are still stuck move on to the next page, and come back to it.

It's best to use a pencil for these exercises so you can correct mistakes if necessary. If you want to challenge yourself, use a ballpoint pen. If you want to get really creative, finish your work with color pencils.

On the next two pages you'll find an example of how to take a random line and draw a subject around it.

SHARK

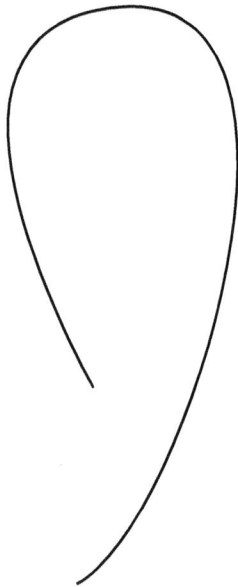

SHARK

DOG

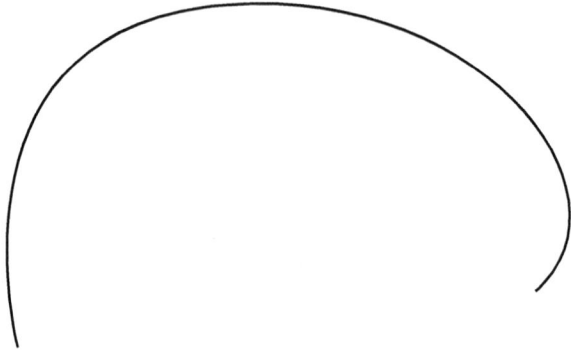

CAT

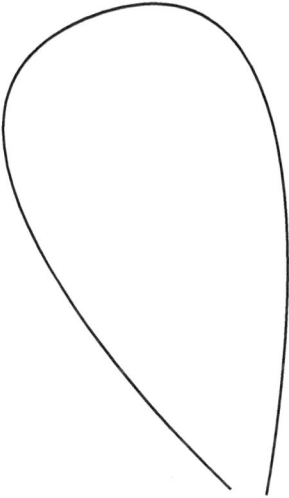

FLOWERS

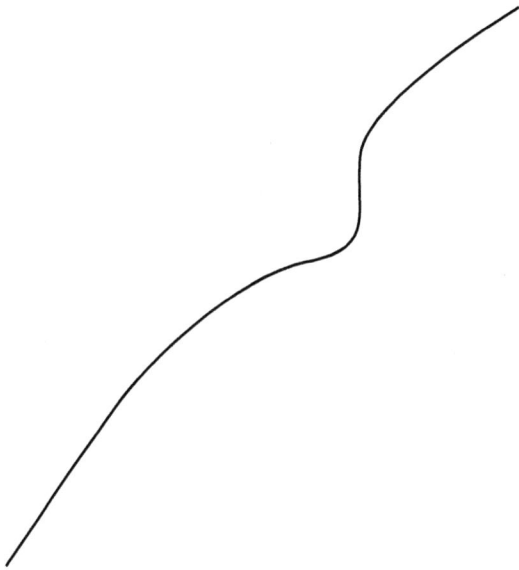

TREE

PENGUIN

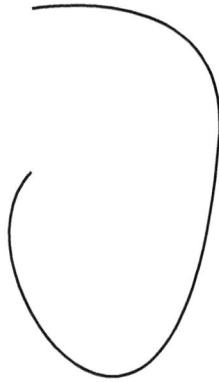

BEAR

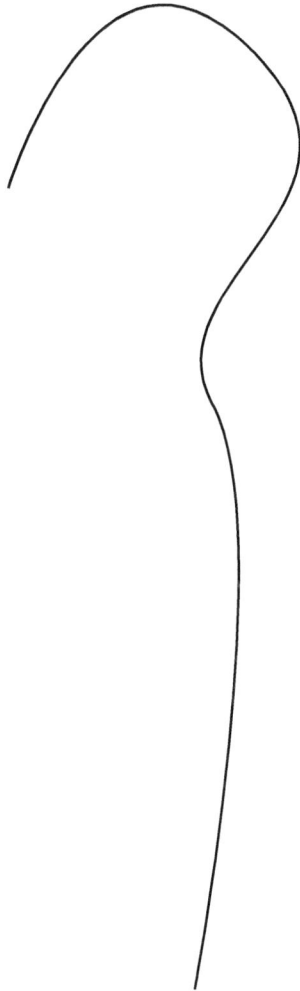

FEATHERS

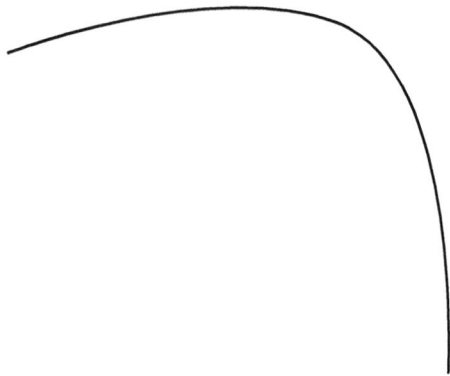

RAT

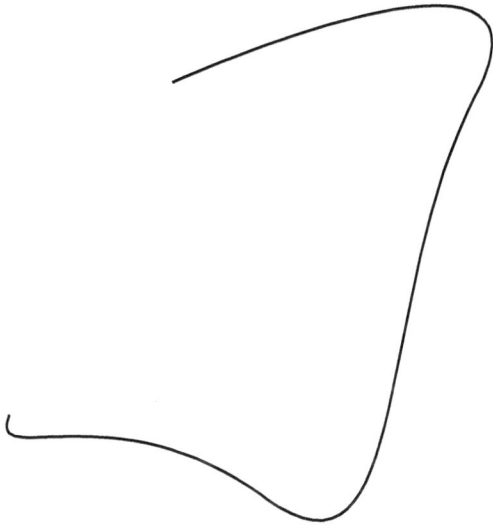

TOOLBOX

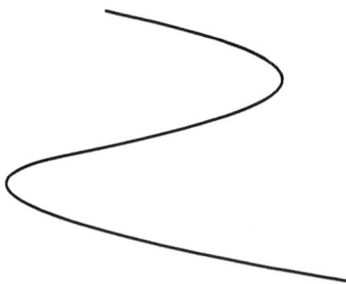

BOOK

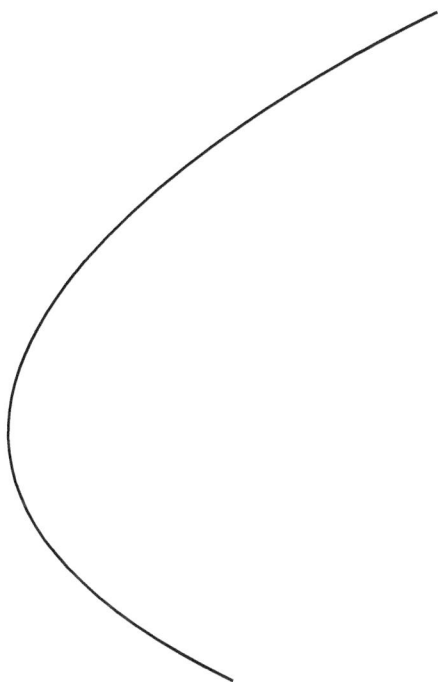

ELEPHANT

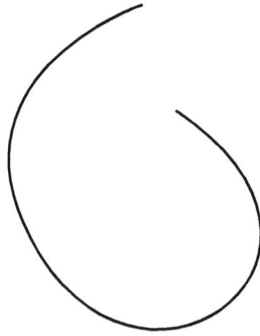

LIZARD

CITY

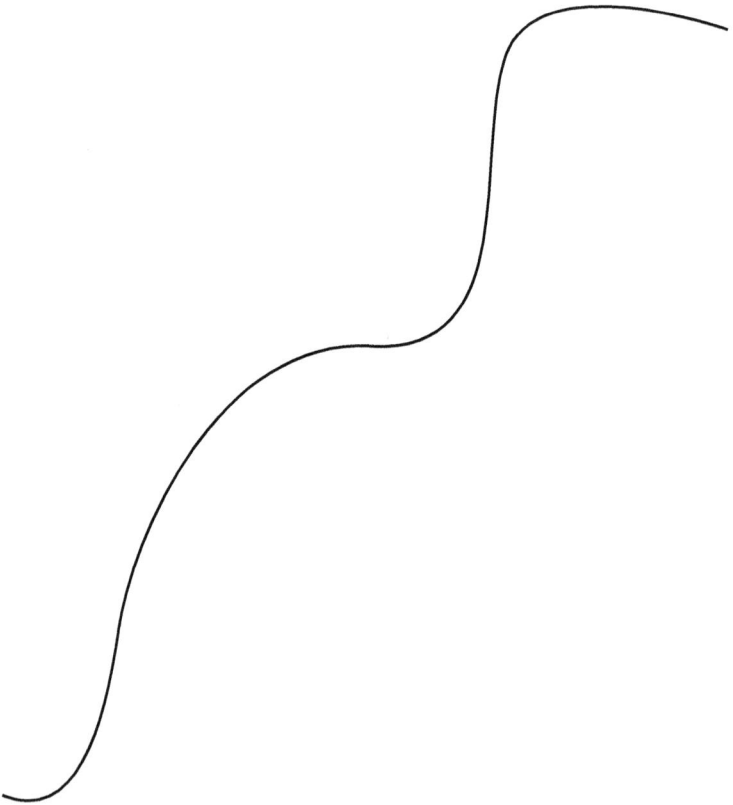

MOUNTAINS

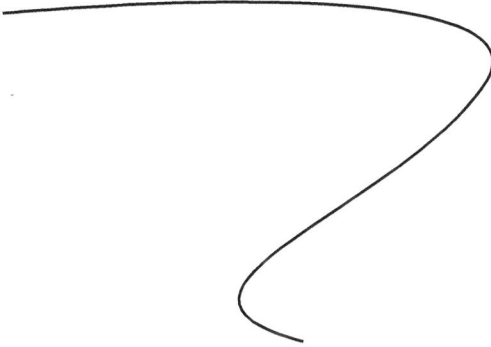

CAMERA

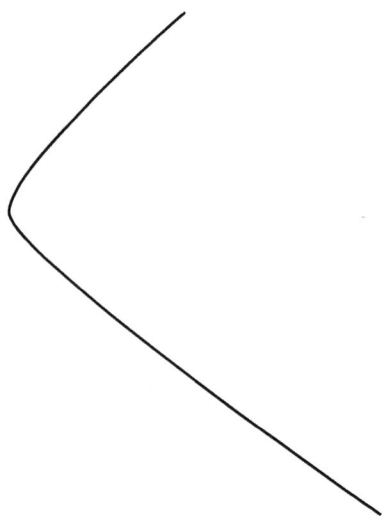

PHOTOGRAPHS

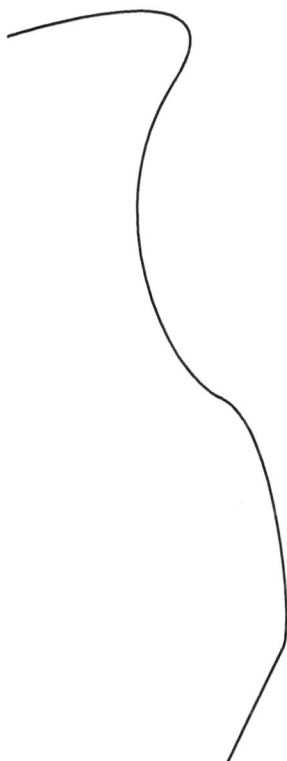

WATCH

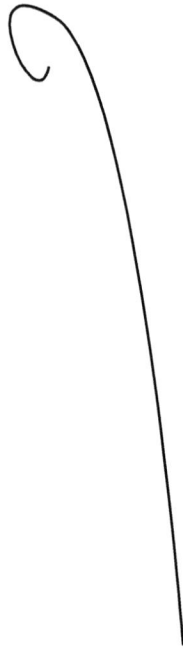

SHOES

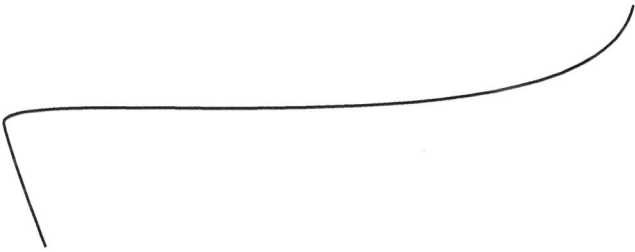

SHIRT

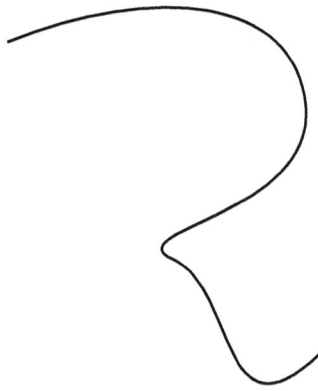

PANTS

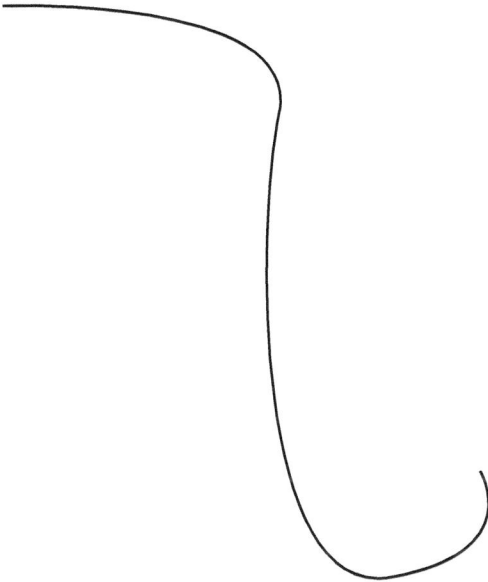

DRESS

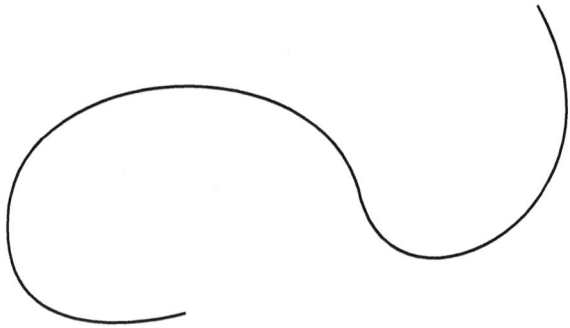

HAT

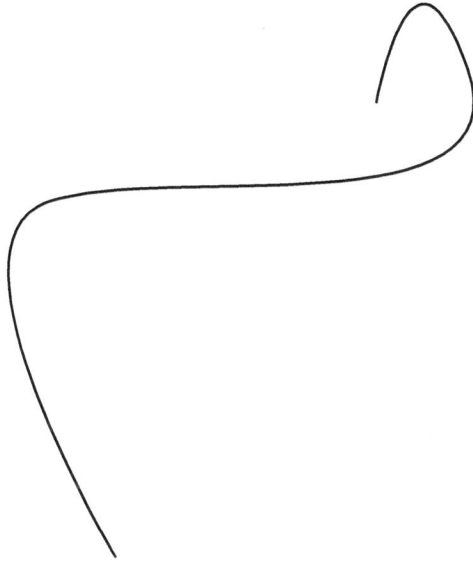

SUNGLASSES

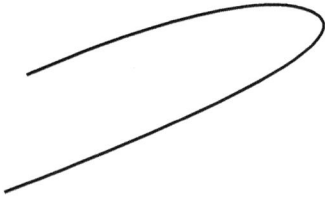

TELEPHONE

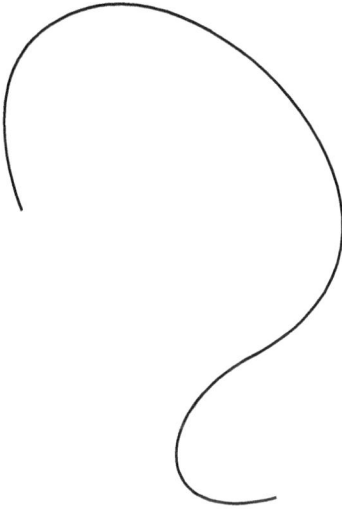

FRUIT

VEGETABLES

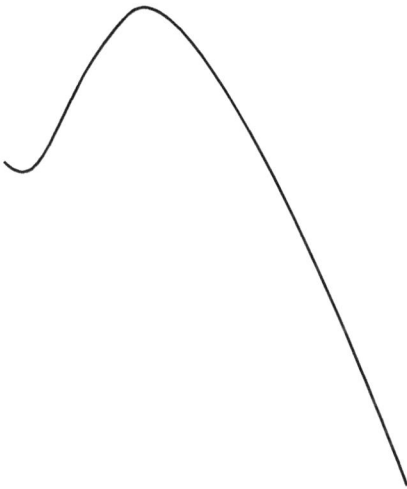

NEWSPAPER

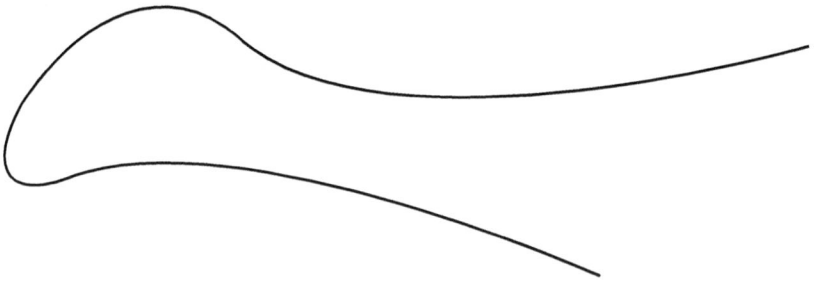

HOUSE

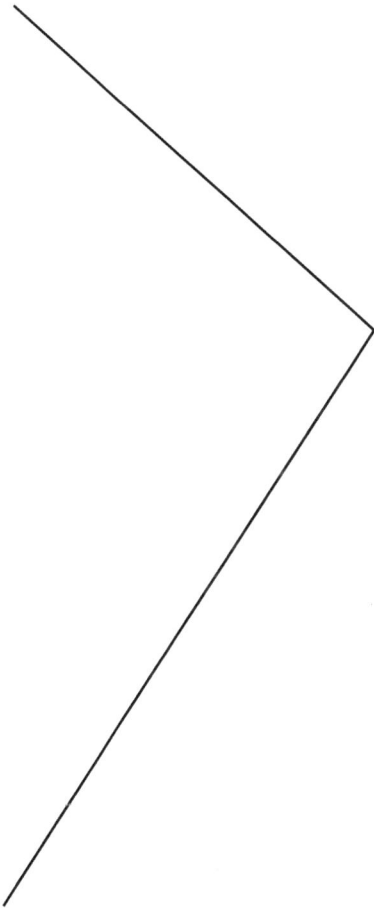

CLOWN

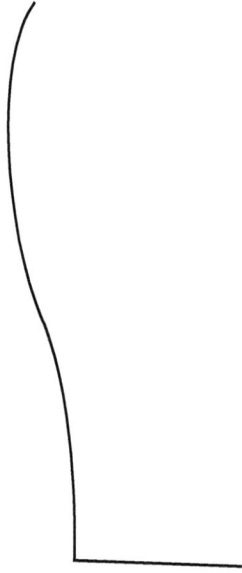

MONKEY

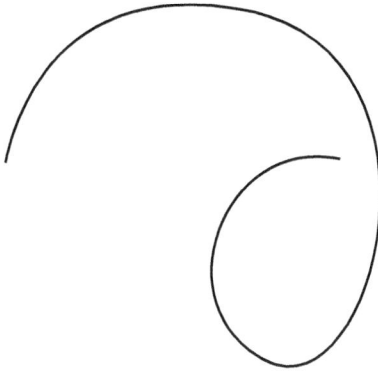

RABBIT

FISH

GIFT

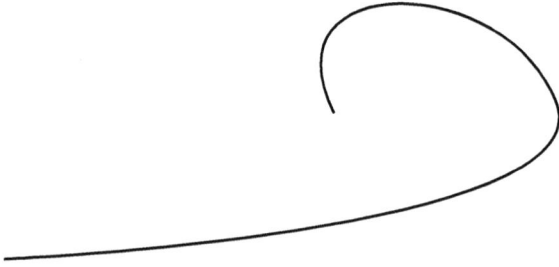

AIRPLANE

BEACH

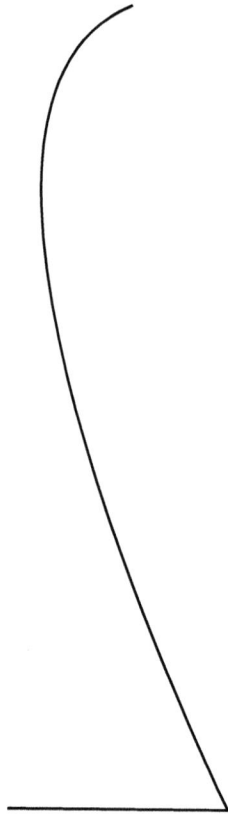

SAILBOAT

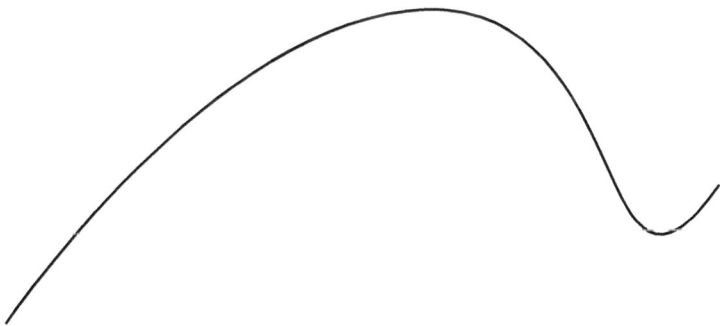

HEADPHONES

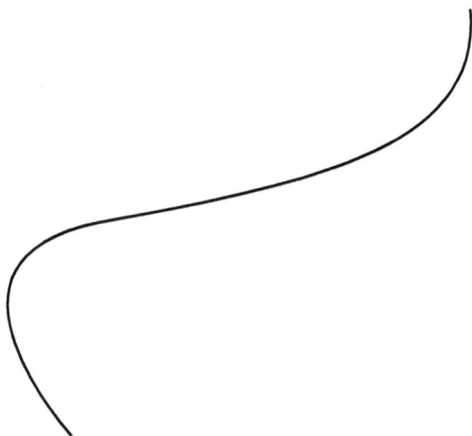

SNAKE

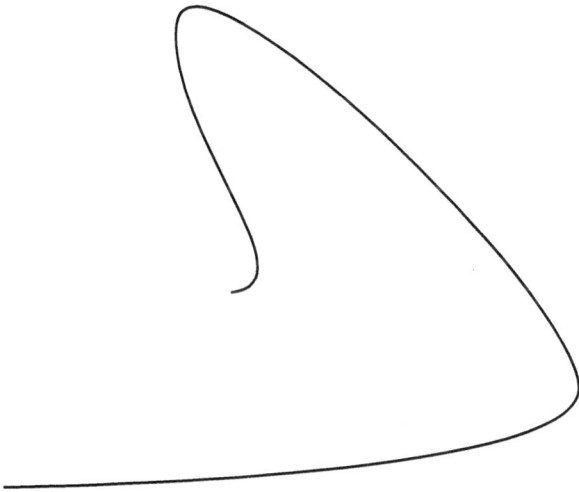

Fox

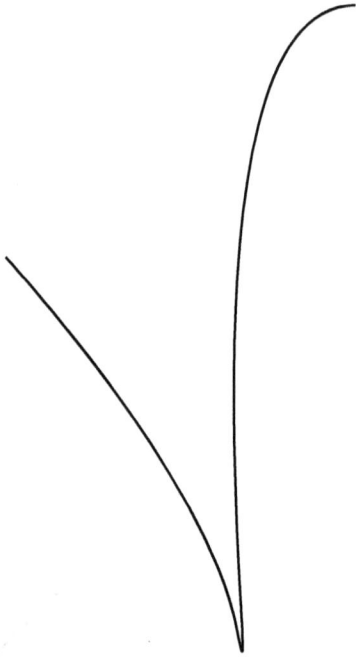

BUTTERFLY

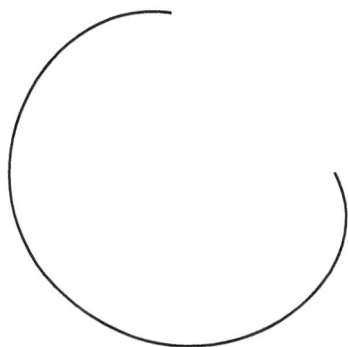

TURTLE

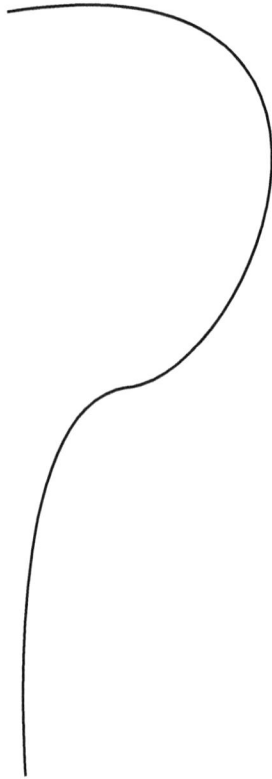

ROBOT

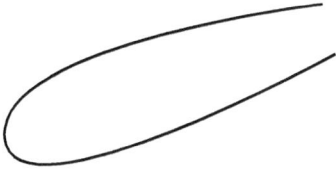

DINOSAUR

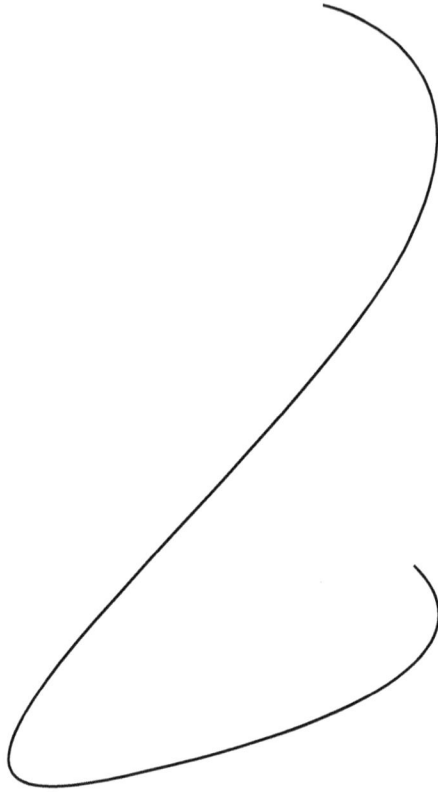

PIRATE SHIP

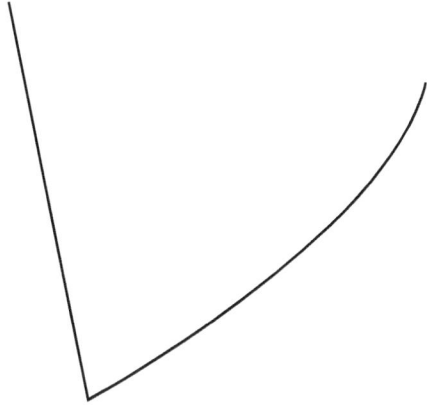

WIZARD

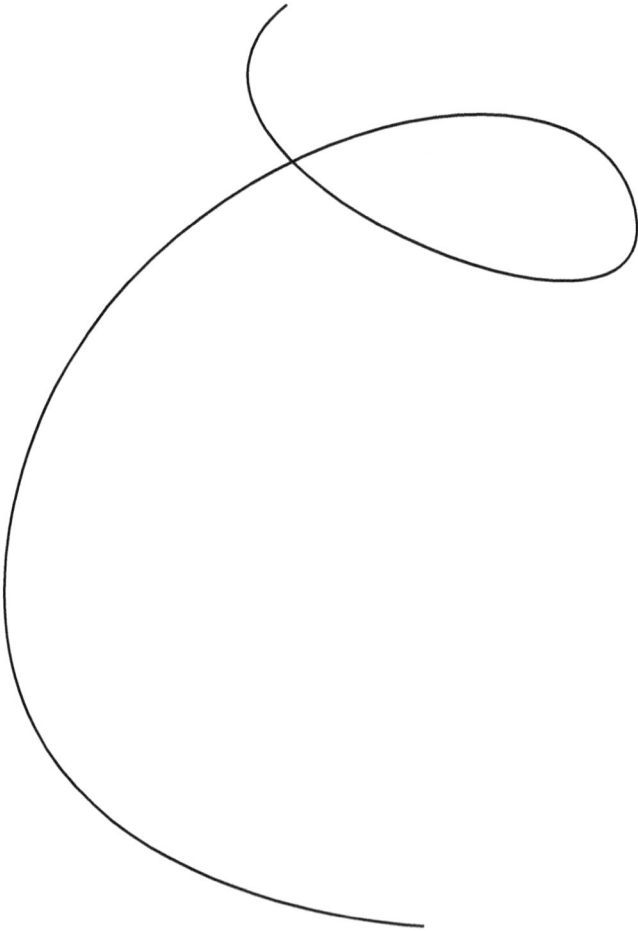

KNIGHT

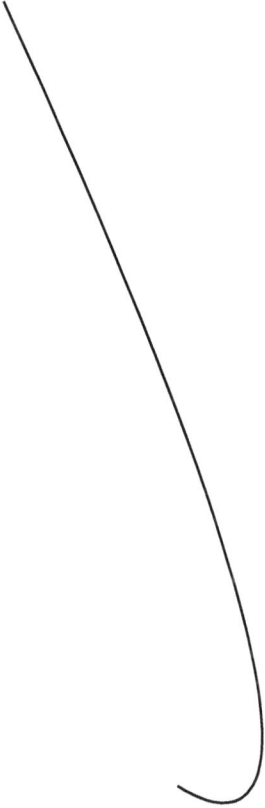

MONSTER

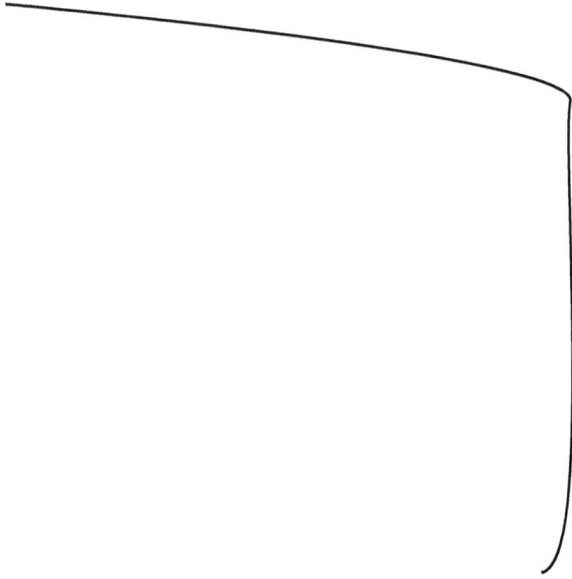

GHOST

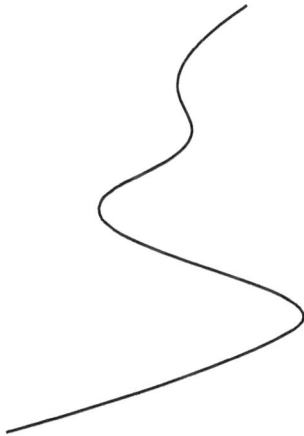

SQUIRREL

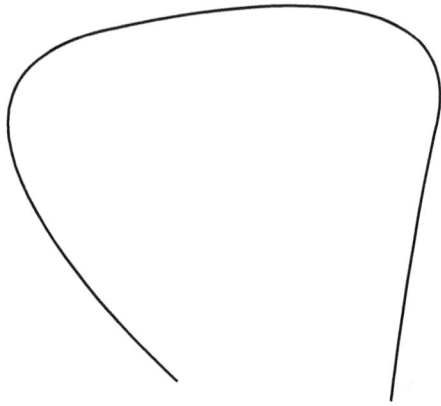

DUCK

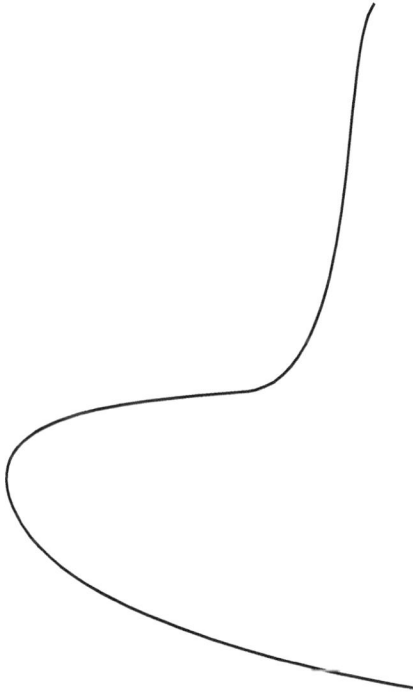

MUSHROOMS

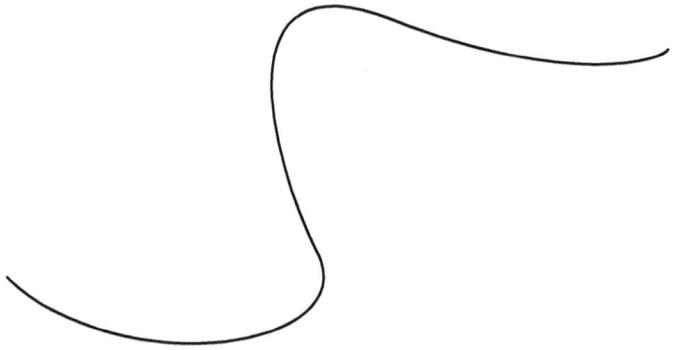

PIG

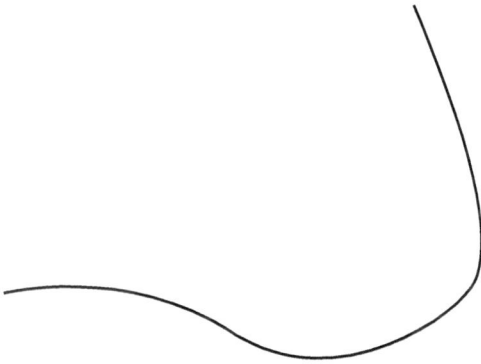

ROLLER COASTER

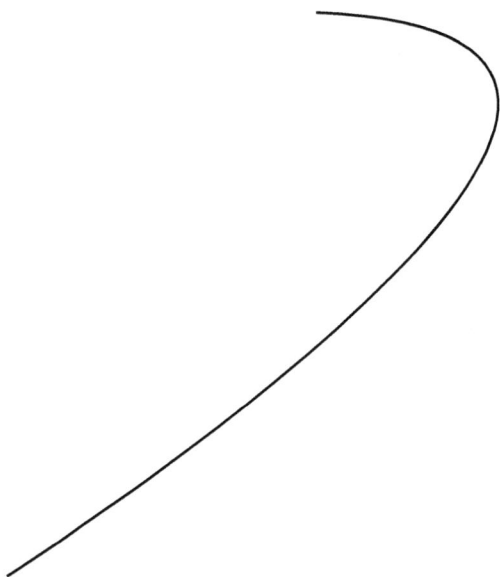

SUBMARINE

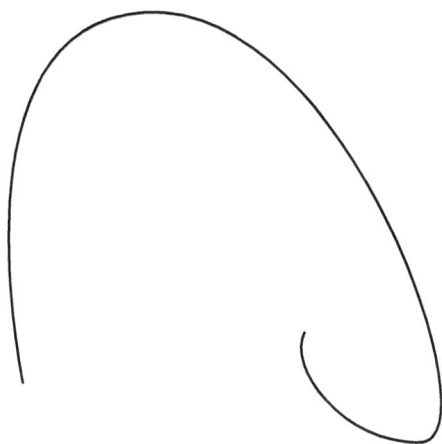

DRAGON

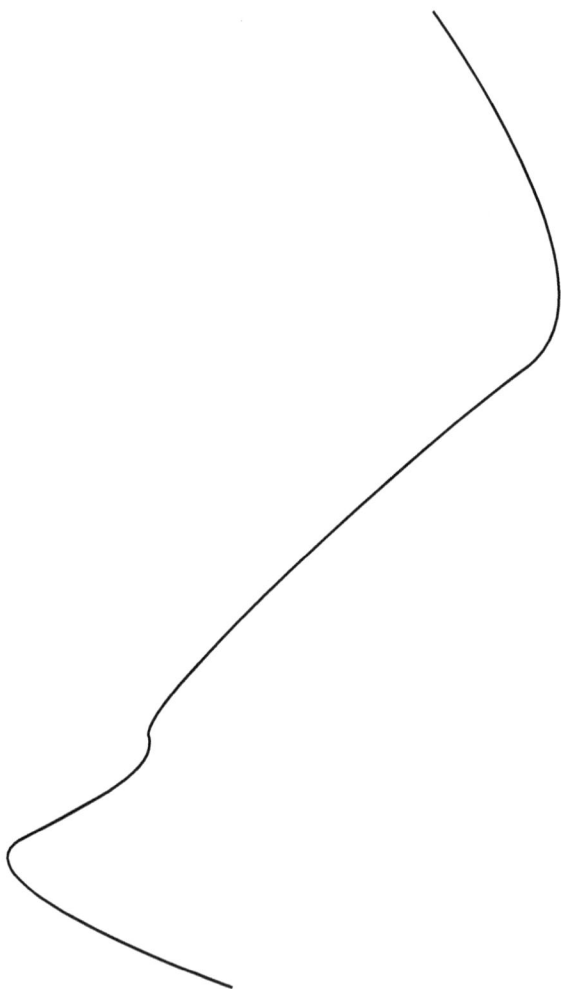

CASTLE

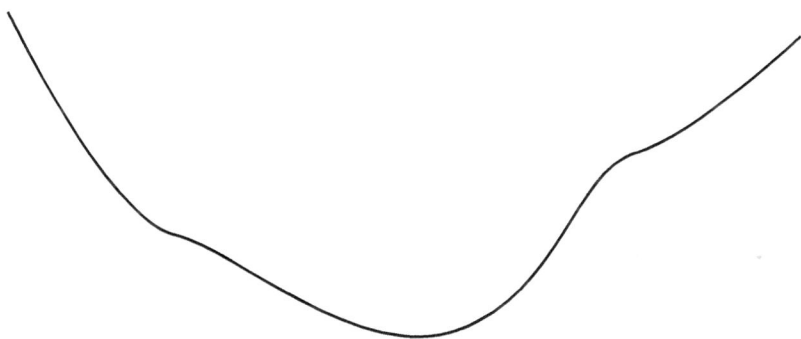

WOMAN

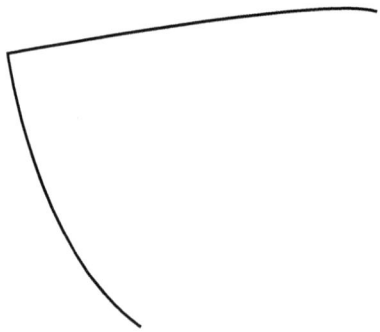

MAN

CAR

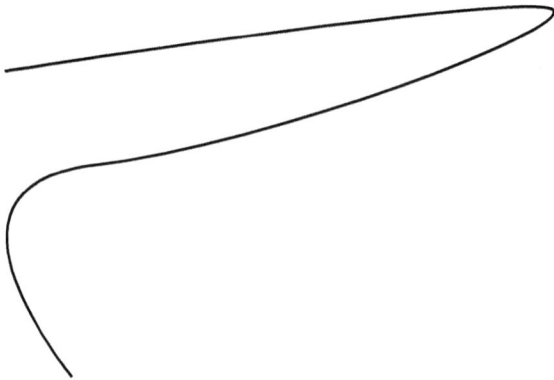

MOTORCYCLE

BASKET

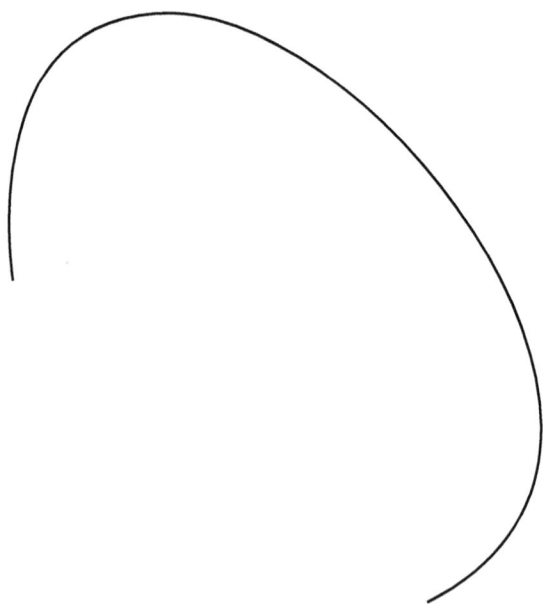

FLAG

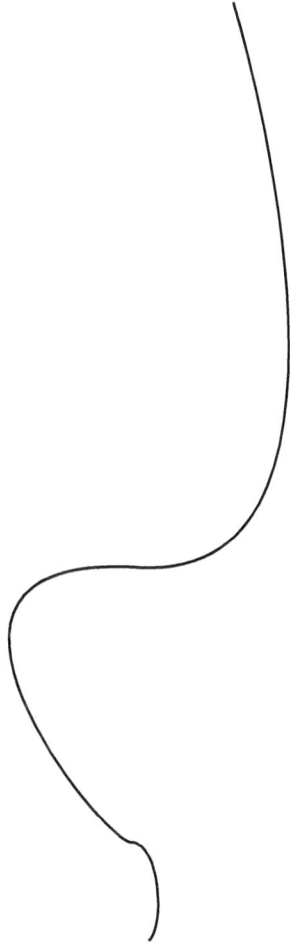

ICE CREAM

TACOS

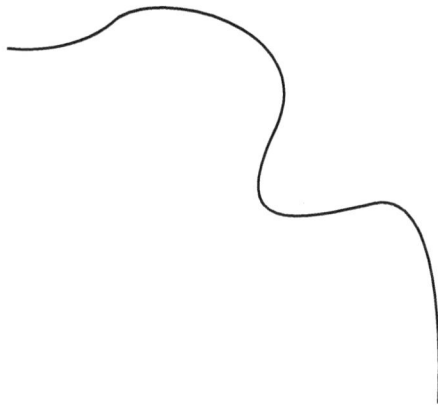

PLAYING CARDS

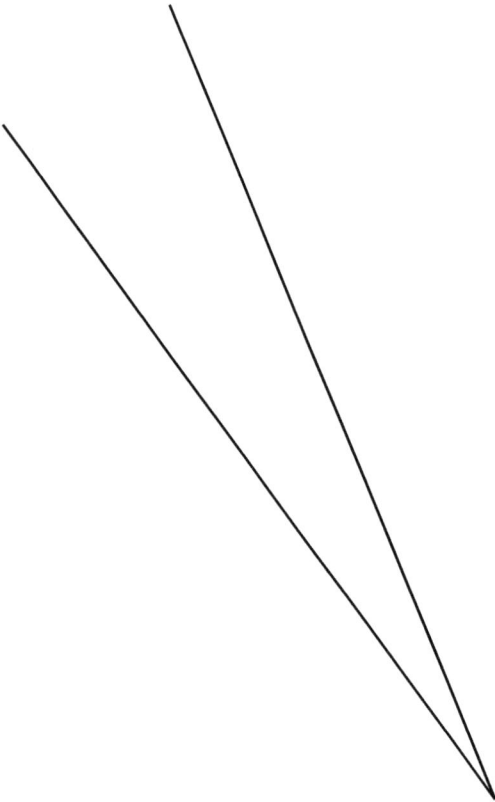

SLOT MACHINE

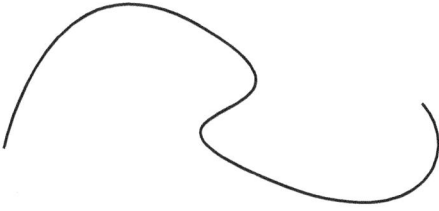

HIPPOPOTAMUS

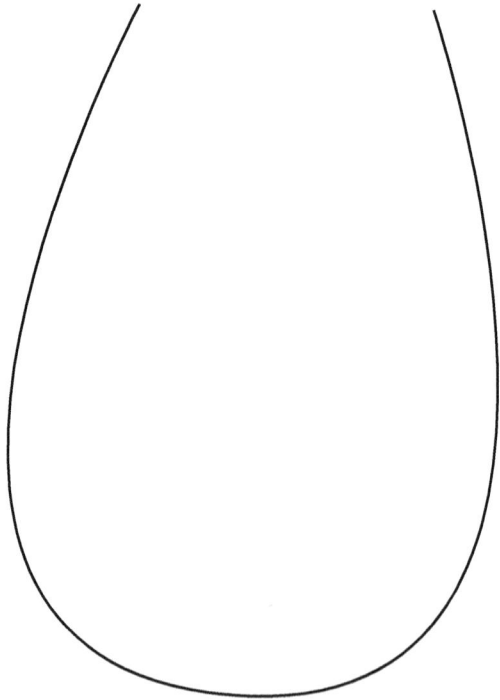

BREAKFAST

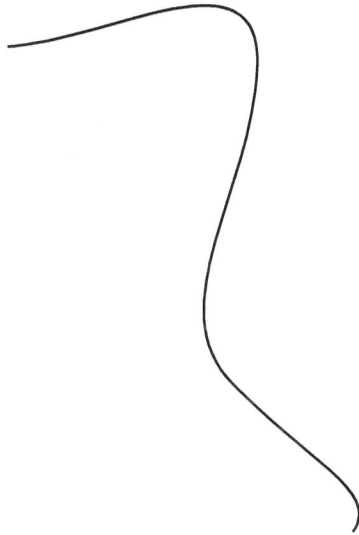

SCORPION

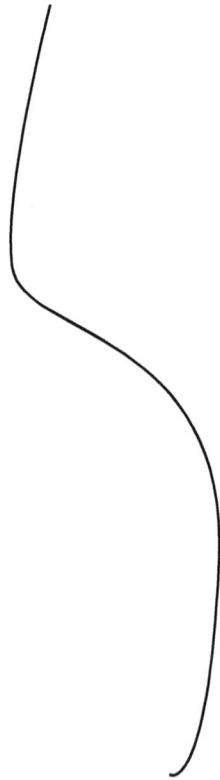

CACTUS

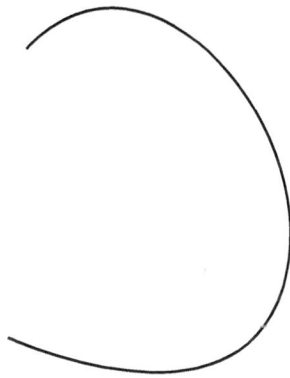

SOCKS

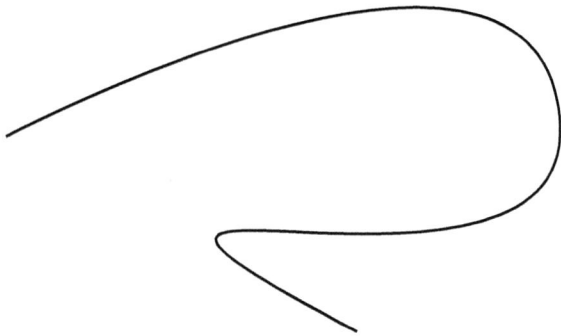

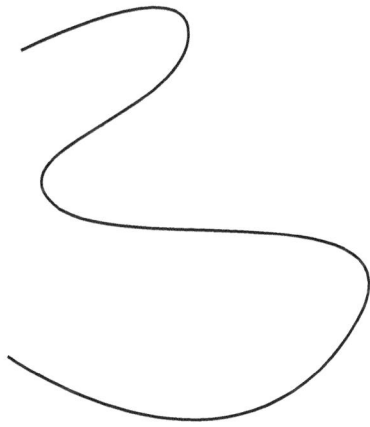

OCTOPUS

SWIMMING POOL

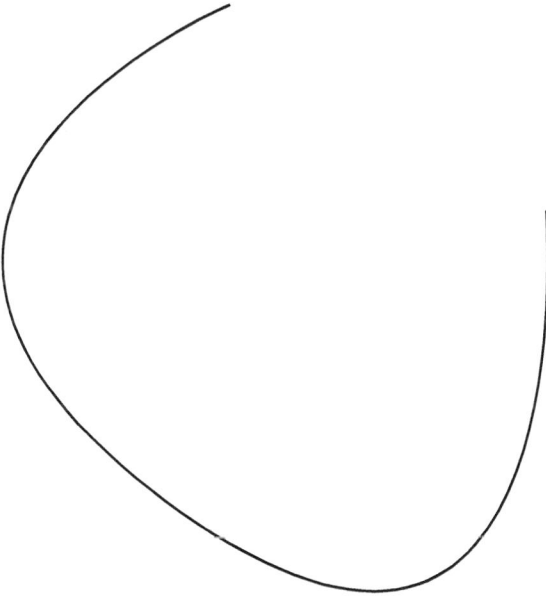

CAKE

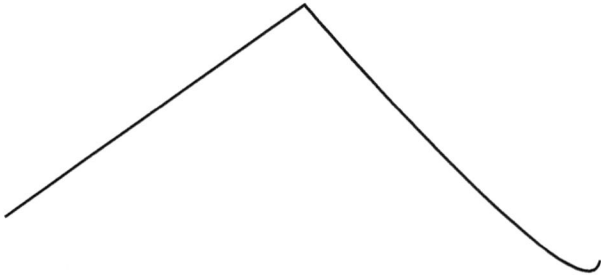

SWIMSUIT

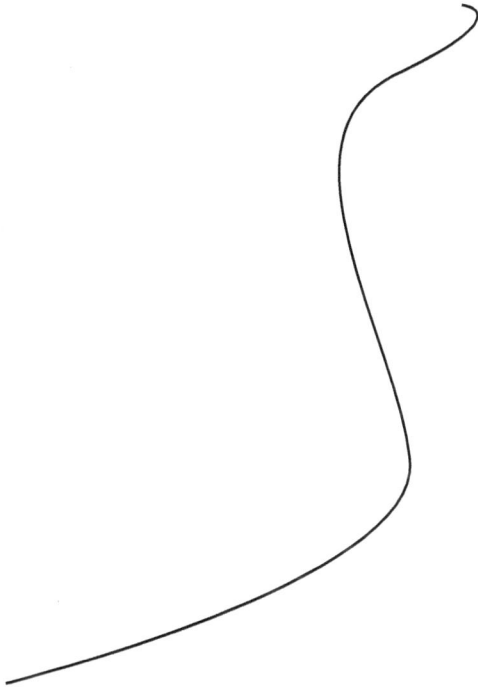

CHURCH

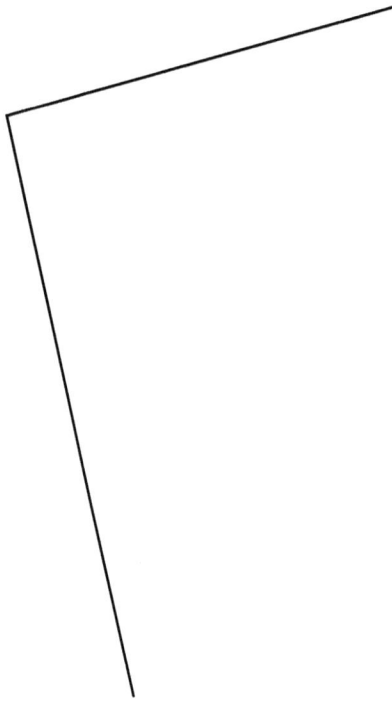

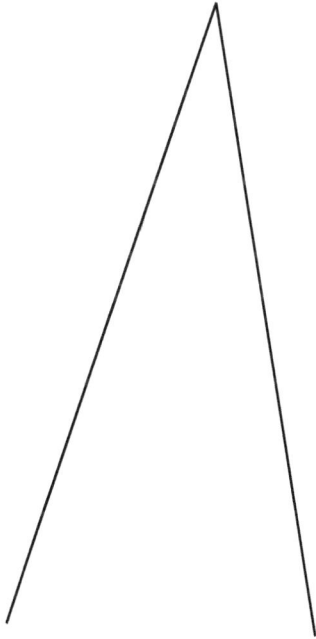

TOASTER

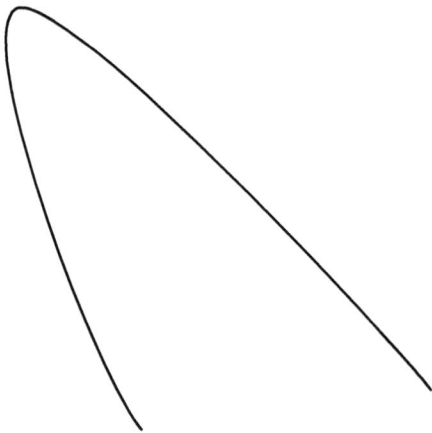

BLENDER

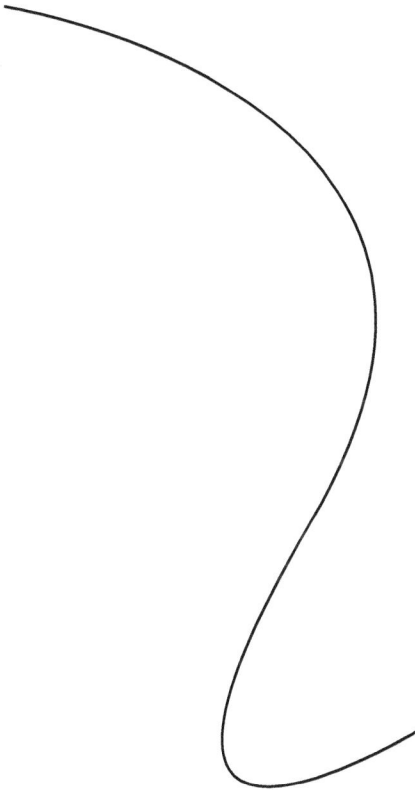

OWL

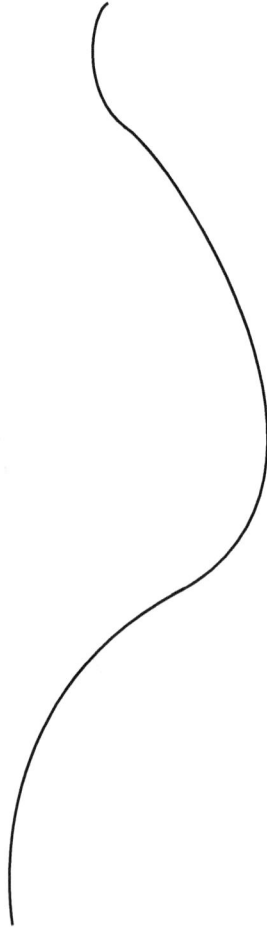

GOAT

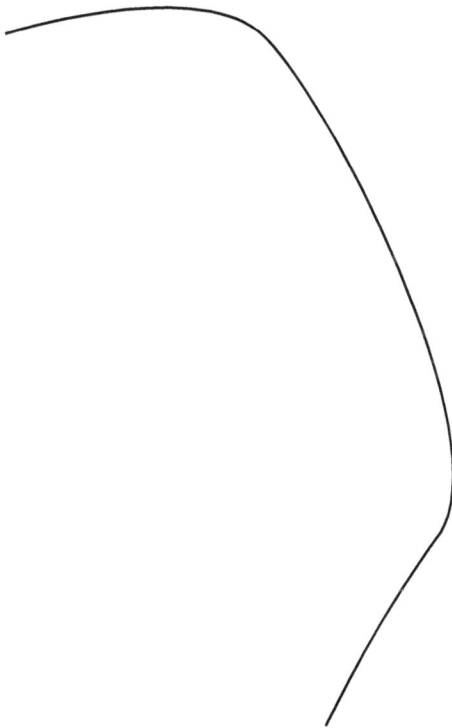

SANDWICH

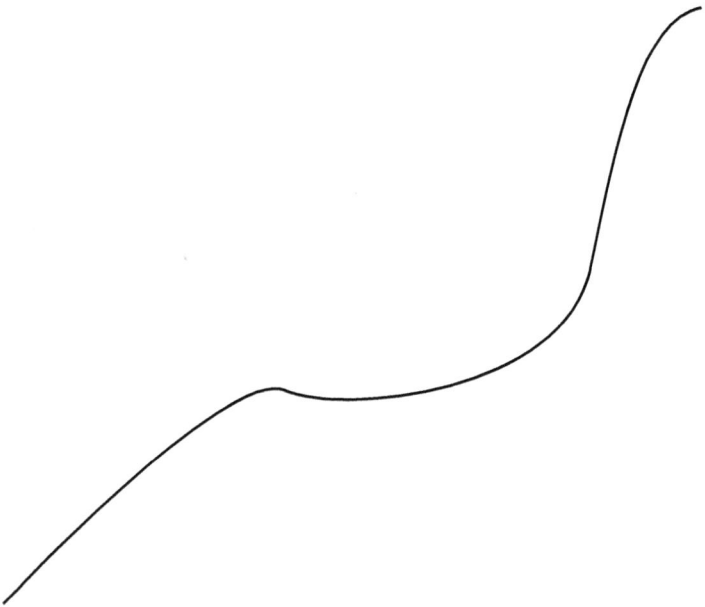

VOLCANO

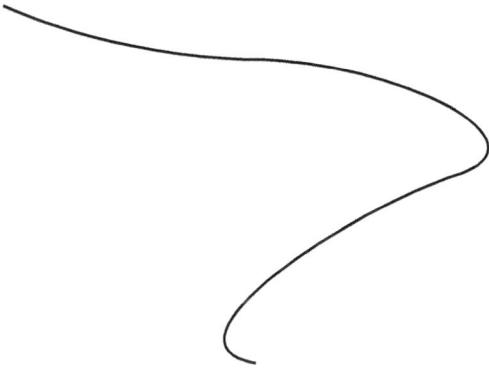

JACKET

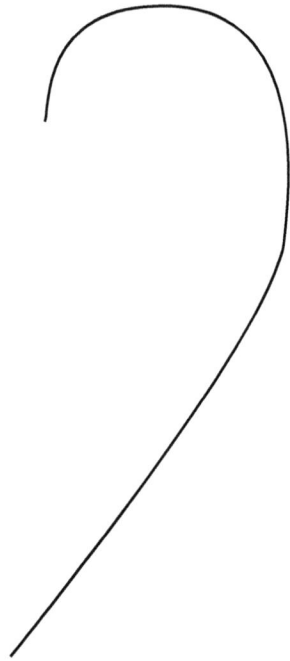

SCARF

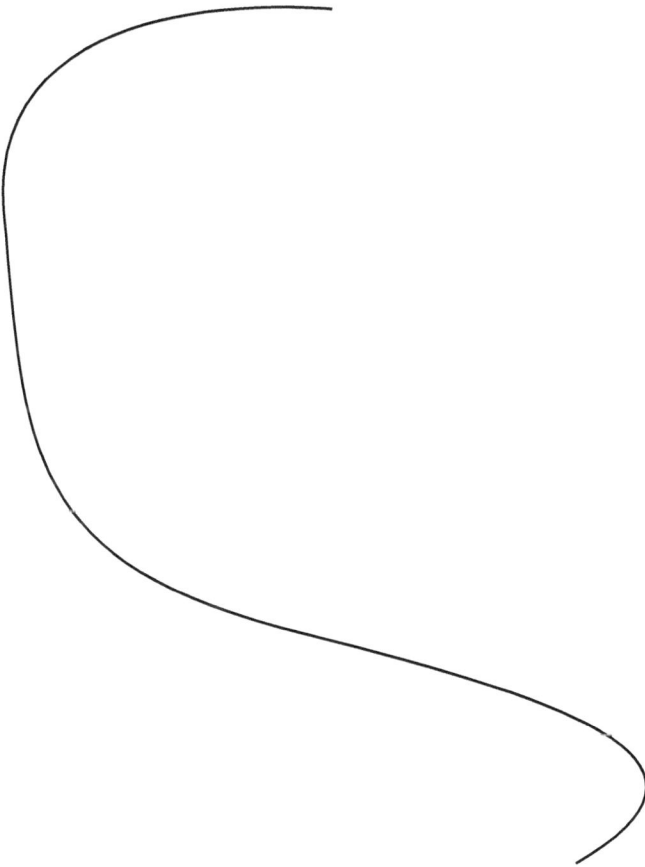

TRAIN

IGLOO

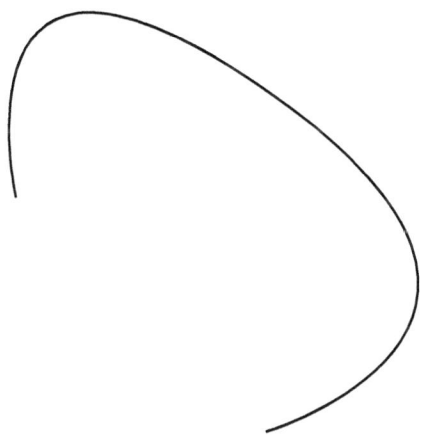

BABY

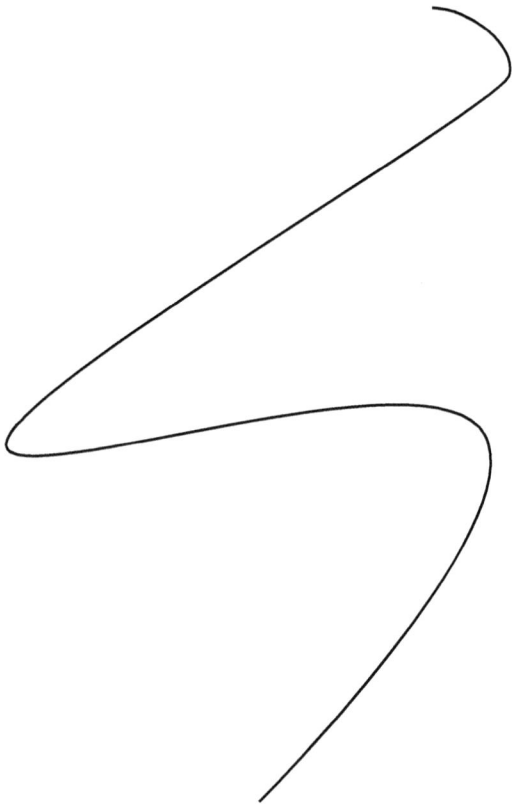

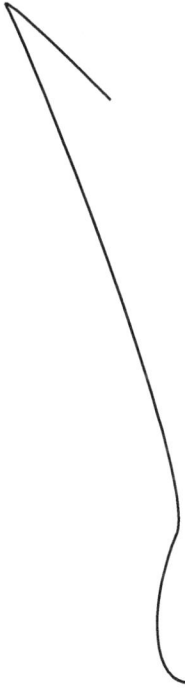

MONEY

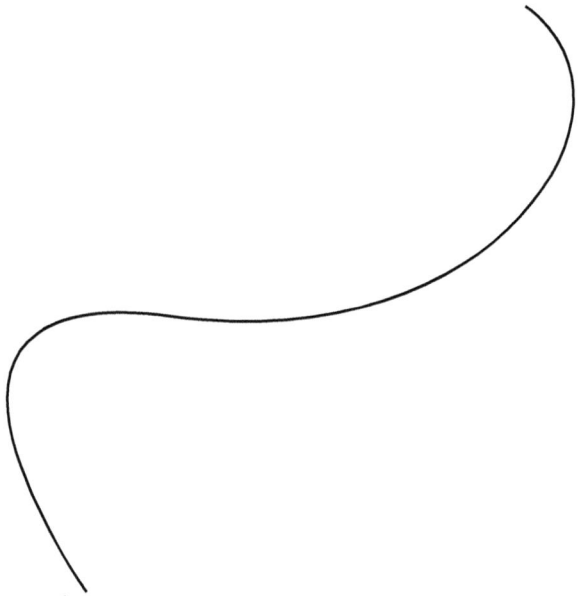

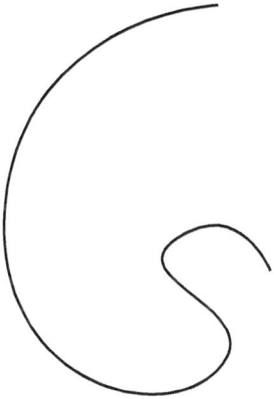

CANYON

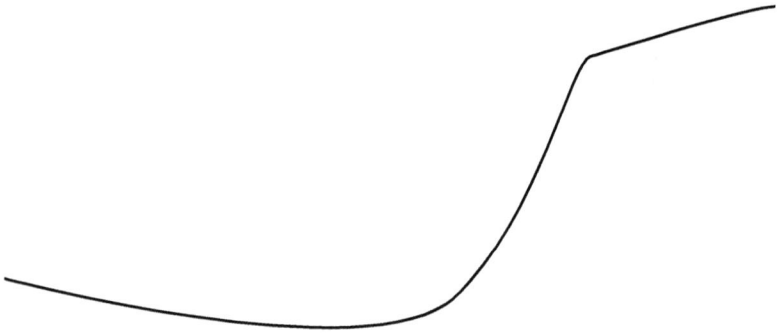

MUMMY

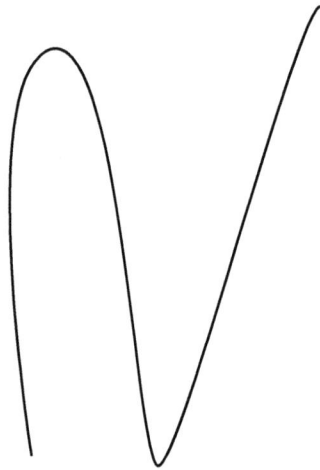

WITCH

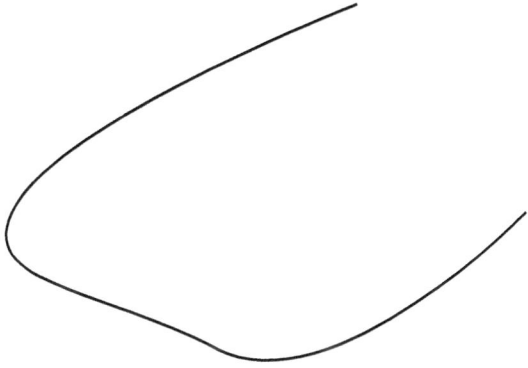

PIANO

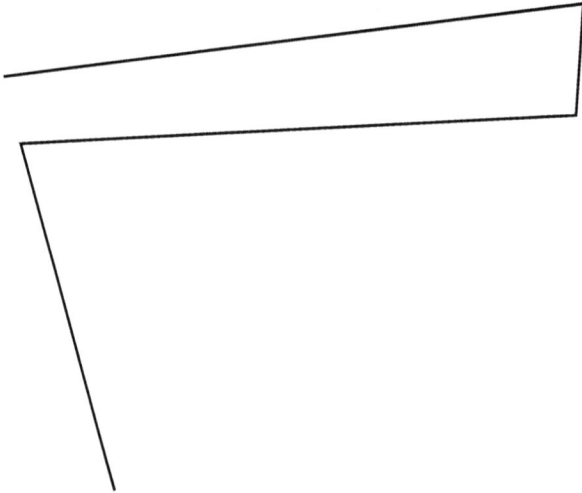

GUITAR

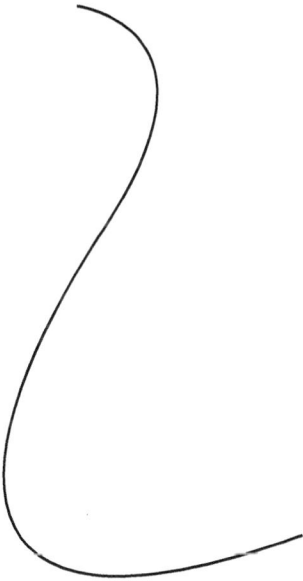

HORN

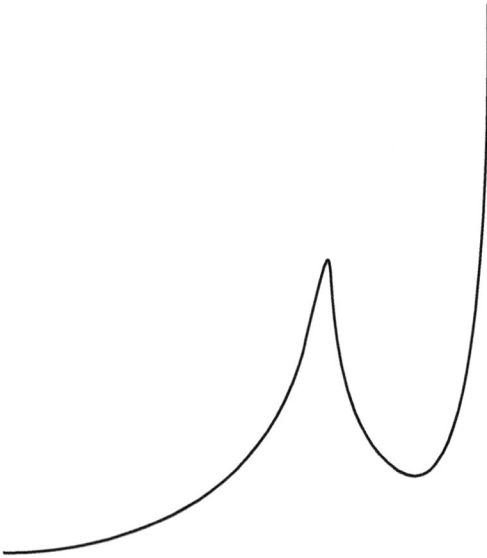

DRUMS

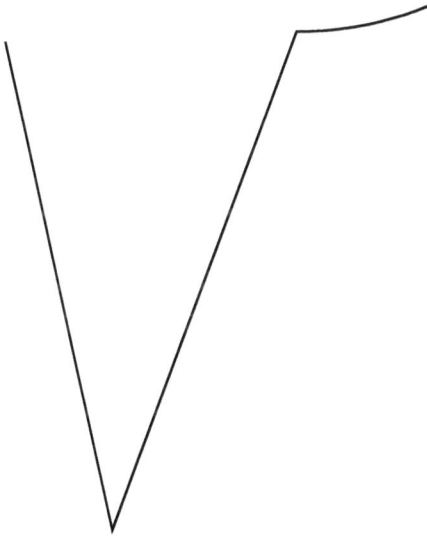

WATERFALL

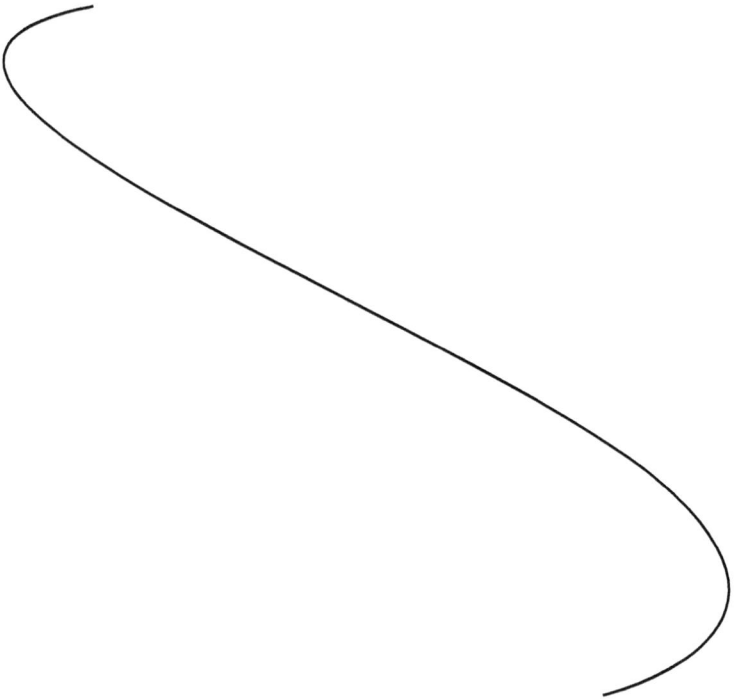

BARN

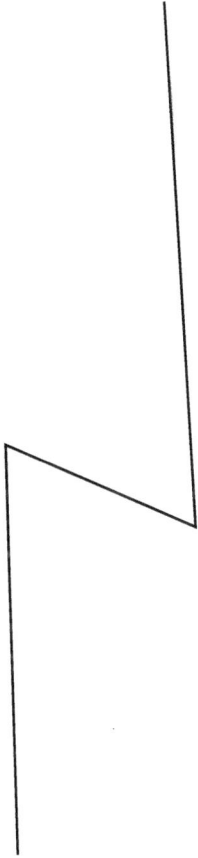

TREASURE CHEST

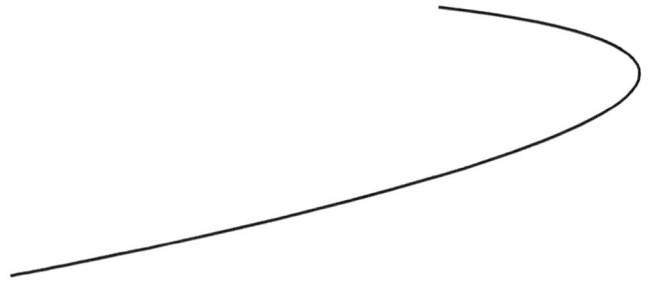

WHALE

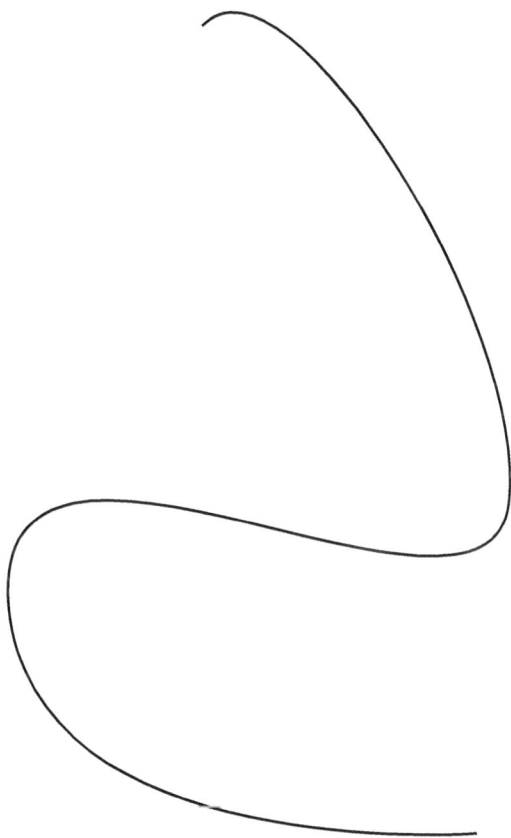

LUNCH BOX

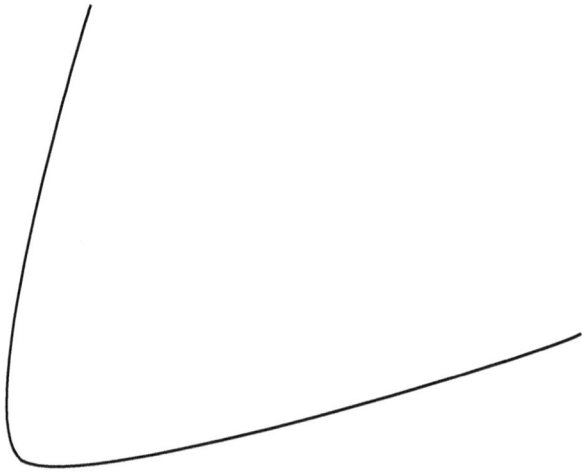

BACKPACK

HELICOPTER

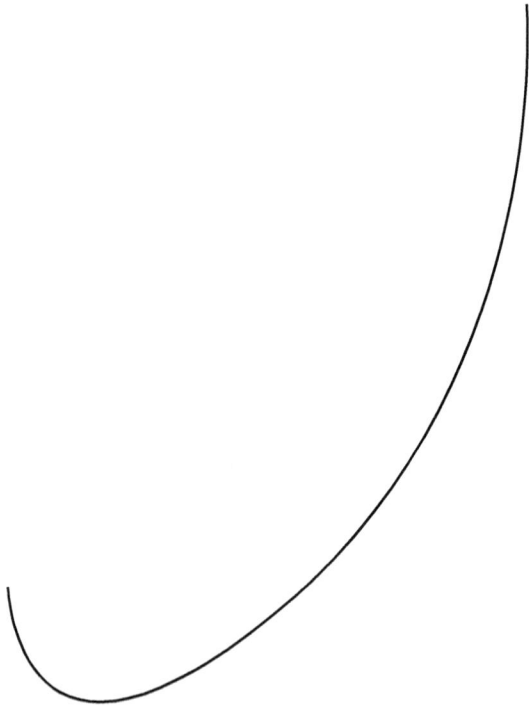

ARMY TANK

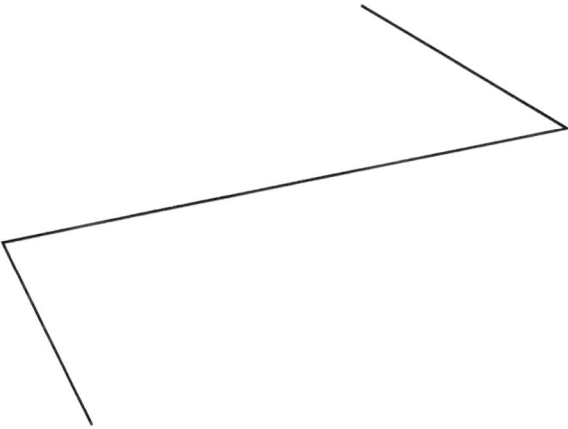

ROCKET

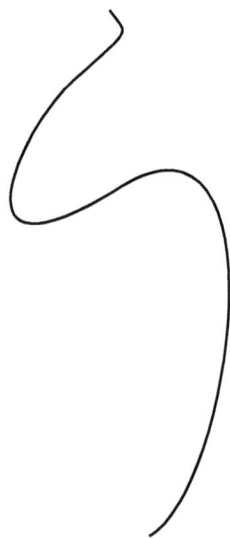

SATELLITE

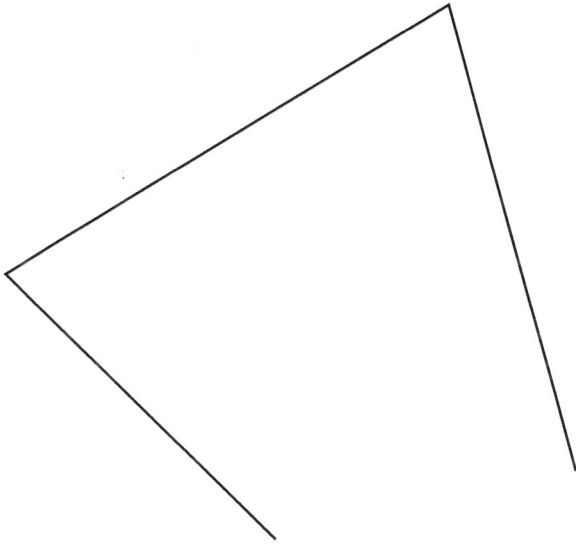

LION

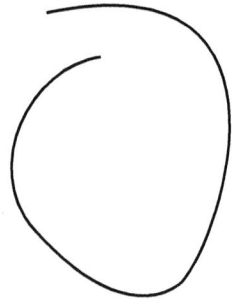

PARROT

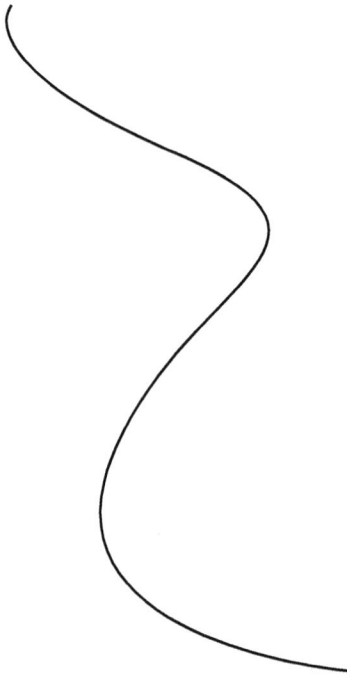

MEN'S HAIRSTYLE

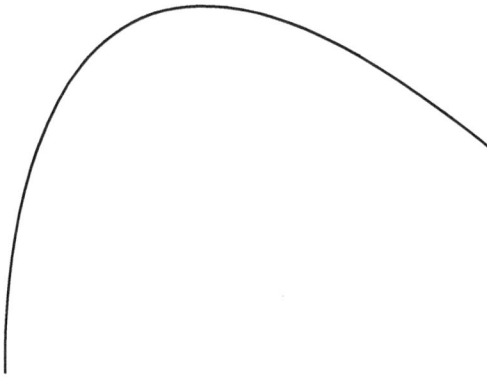

WALLET

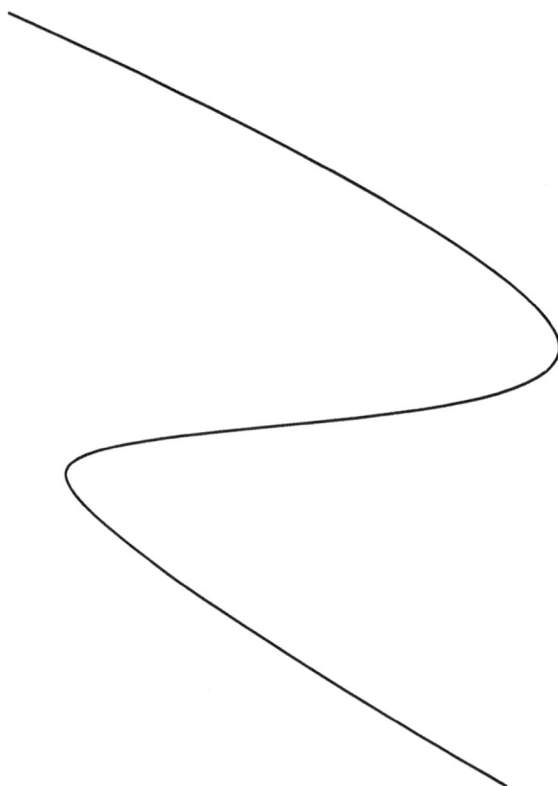

PURSE

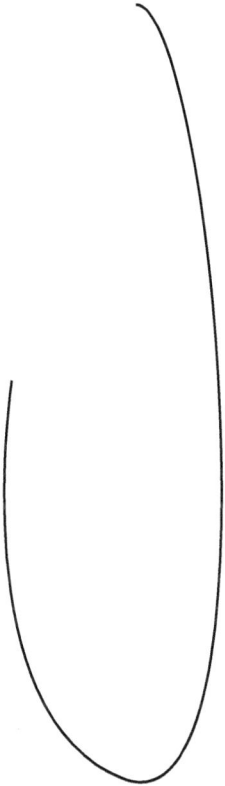

ASTRONAUT

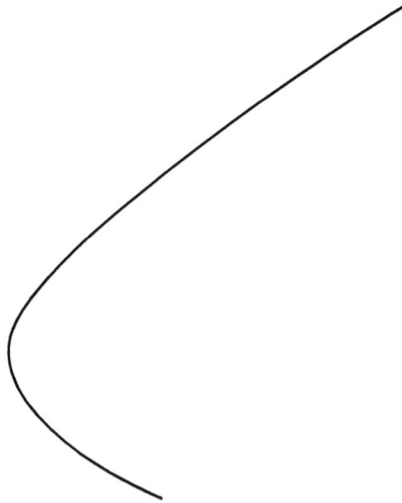

COWBOY

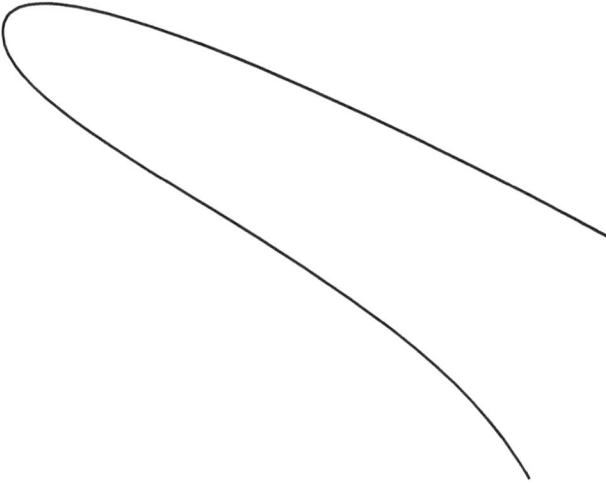

EAGLE

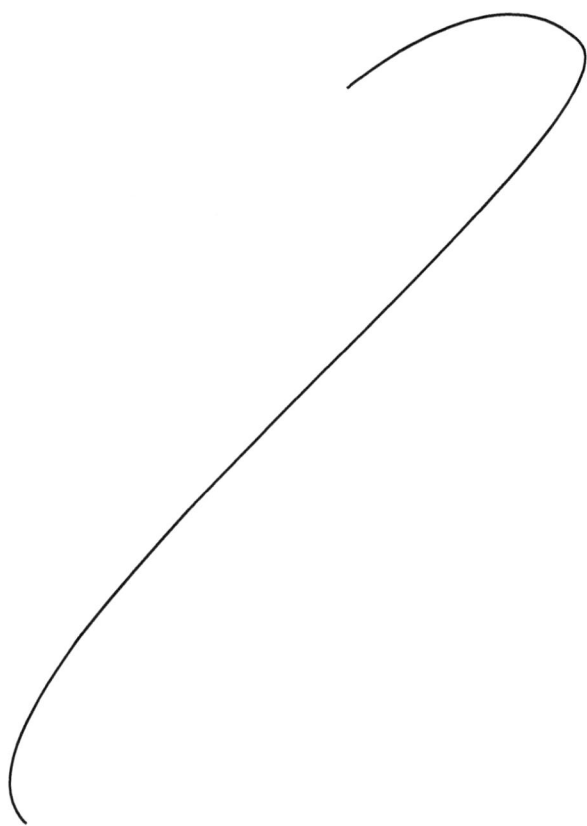

SEAL

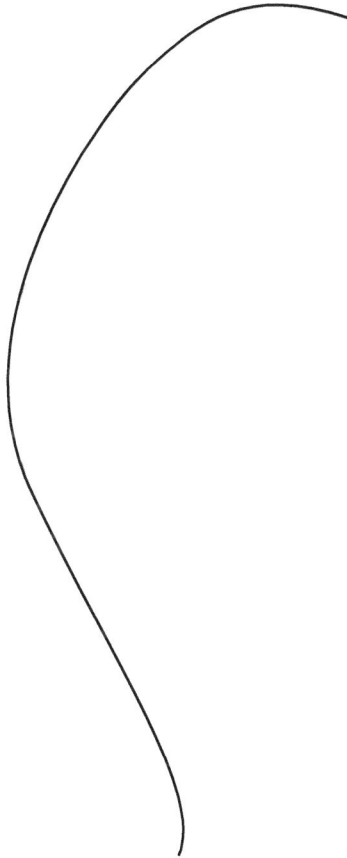

COMPUTER

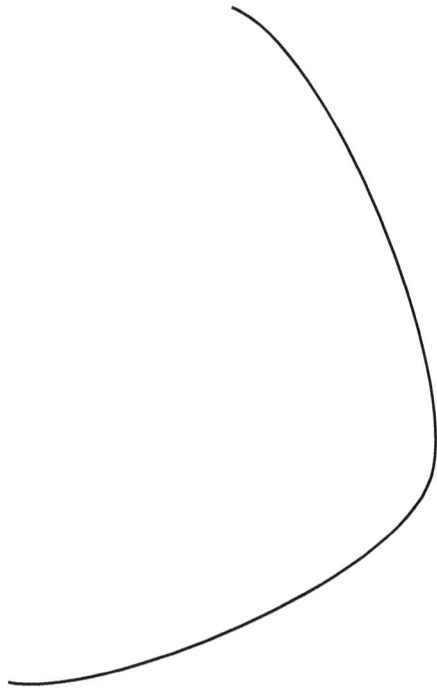

SPIDER

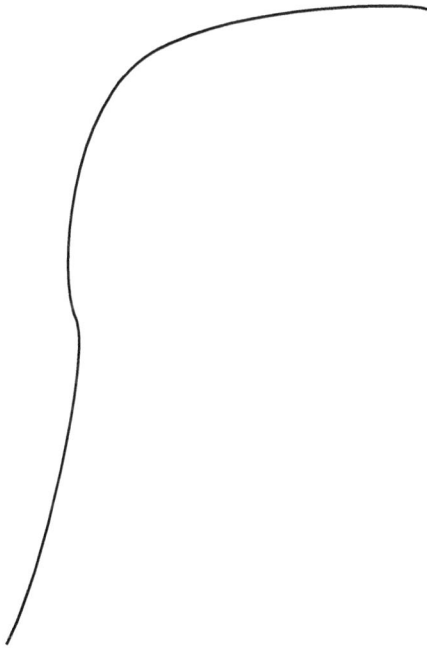

WEDDING DRESS

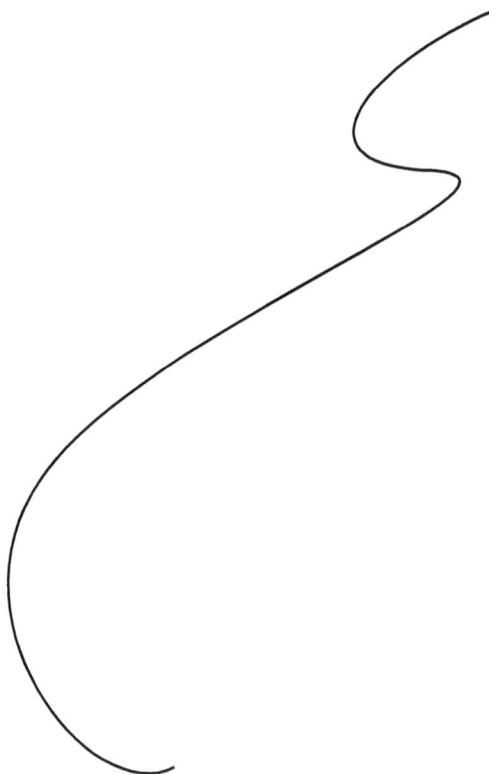

FIREPLACE

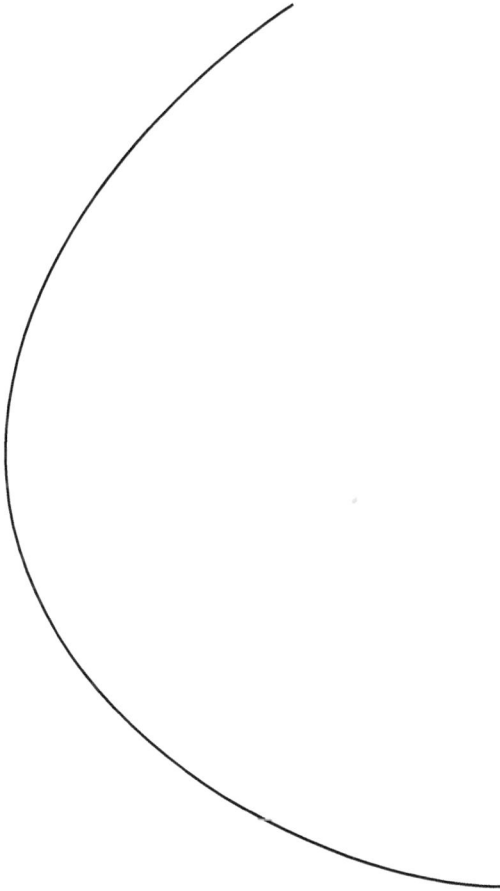